5-a-Day, Every Day

By

Dr. Farah Alam-Mirza, MRCGP, DCH, DRCOG, DFSRH, MBBS, PG Certificate in Teaching in Primary Care

Illustrations by Yunzila Mirza

One morning, Sofiya was having breakfast.

"Sofiya, have your cereal, please," said Dad.

"I don't like cereal!" said Sofiya. "I'll have an egg instead."

"Cereal is good for you," said Dad. "Finish your juice, please."

"I'm done," replied Sofiya, and she ran off.

Later, at school, the bell sounded for lunch.

"Let's go and eat," said Theo. "I am so hungry!"

In the lunch hall, the dinner lady asked, "Would you like any greens, Theo?"

"Yes, please," replied Theo. "I'll have some broccoli and peas. I love my greens!"

"How about you, Sofiya?" asked the dinner lady.

"Ugh! I don't like greens!" said Sofiya.

"Greens are good for you," said the dinner lady.

"No, thanks," said Sofiya. "I'll have some chips, please."

The next day, Sofiya and Theo went to Uncle Phil's to play football.

They had a great time with their friend, Aanshi.

Aunty Sonia brought out a tray of milk and fruit. "Come along, kids! It's time for tea!" she called.

The children came eagerly.

"Ooh, strawberries, my favourite!" said Aanshi.

"Can I have an apple, please?" said Theo.

"Of course you can," said Aunty Sonia, as she handed out the fruit.

The children grabbed the fruit and ate hungrily, but Sofiya didn't want any.

"How about you, Sofiya?" asked Uncle Phil.

"I don't like fruit," said Sofiya.

"I want some chocolate!" she said, grabbing a bar of chocolate as she ran back to Theo and Aanshi.

Later on at home, Sofiya was not feeling so well.

"My tummy hurts!" she told Dad.

"Do you need to go to the toilet?" asked Dad.

"I'll try and go," replied Sofiya, and she went to the toilet.

A little while later, Sofiya came back.

"How are you feeling now?" asked Dad.

"My tummy hurts and my poo is so hard!" cried Sofiya.

"We had better go to the doctor," said Dad.

"What brings you in today, Sofiya?" asked Dr. Alam.

"My tummy hurts and my poo is very hard," replied Sofiya.

"How long has it been going on?" asked Dr. Alam.

"A few weeks now," said Dad.

"How many glasses of water do you drink in a day, Sofiya?" asked Dr. Alam.

Sofiya thought about it. "Maybe two glasses," she said.

"And do you eat fruits and vegetables?" said Dr. Alam.

Sofiya looked at Dad "Uh oh!" she said. "I don't like that stuff!"

"Sofiya is a fussy eater," added Dad.

"If you don't drink enough water and eat enough fruits and vegetables, your poo can become hard and give you a tummy ache," said Dr. Alam.

"You need to drink at least seven glasses of water a day," she explained, "and have five portions of fruits and vegetables. Cereals and wholemeal bread are good, too."

"If you do that, your poo will become soft and it won't hurt," said Dr. Alam. "Do you think you can do that, Sofiya?"

"Yes, I can," said Sofiya. "I want to get better!"

"Fantastic!" said Dr. Alam. "Let me know how you get on."

The next morning, Dad asked, "What would you like for breakfast, Sofiya?"

"I'll have some cereal!" replied Sofiya.

As she left for school, Sofiya grabbed a juicy red apple.

"Yummy! This is delicious!" she said. "Now I'm going to have my five-a-day every day!"

Question time!

1. How many portions of fruit and vegetables should you eat in a day?

2. How many glasses of water should you drink in a day?

3. What happened to Sofiya when she didn't eat enough greens?

Answers

1. Five

2. Seven

3. Her poo became hard and she had a tummy ache.

About this book

The aim of this series is to promote awareness and wellbeing in children, to prevent disease and illness, and to encourage a healthy lifestyle in a fun and interactive way.

Disclaimer

This book is for educational purposes only. It is not meant to be a substitute for professional medical advice. Always seek the advice of your doctor if you are unwell.

Health Promotion Series

Other books in the series available on Amazon:

"Wash Your Hands"

"Ouch, I Need a Plaster!"

"Drink Up"

"Achoo! Catch it! Bin it! Kill it!"

"An Itchy Round Rash"

"Brush Your Teeth"

"Sunkissed"

"Worms Away"